The Crow Killer

"Liver-Eating" Jeremiah Johnson

Vigilante Vengeance Run Amok

Jack Smith

All rights reserved. © 2022 by Jack Smith and Maplewood Publishing. No part of this publication or the information in it may be quoted from or reproduced in any form by means such as printing, scanning, photocopying, or otherwise without prior written permission of the copyright holder.

Efforts have been made to ensure that the information in this book is accurate and complete. However, the author and the publisher do not warrant the accuracy of the information, text, and graphics contained within the book due to the rapidly changing nature of science, research, known and unknown facts, and the internet. The author and the publisher do not hold any responsibility for errors, omissions, or contrary interpretation of the subject matter herein. This book is presented solely for motivational and informational purposes only.

Warning
Throughout the book, there are some descriptions of murders and crime scenes that some people might find disturbing. There might be also some language used by people involved in the murders that may not be appropriate.

Note
Words in italic are quoted words from verbatim and have been reproduced as is, including any grammatical errors and misspelled words.

ISBN 9798447702069

Printed in the United States

Contents

The Crow Killer - How It All Began   1

John Johnson First sets Out on His Own   3

In the Big Blue Country   7

Back at Hatcher's Old Homestead   13

Crazy Woman and Tragic Mountain Magic   17

The Mountain Man and the Swan   23

The Vendetta Begins   27

And the Vendetta Continues…   33

The Crow Killer Captured…   39

But Not for Long   39

The Last Crow and the Last Batch of Biscuits for the Road   47

The Life He Led - In Final Consideration of the Crow Killer   53

The Crow Killer
How It All Began

The individual who comes down to us as the "Crow Killer" was a simple trapper who lived in the Rocky Mountains in the mid-19th century. In other words, he was a "mountain man." Even by the standards of the mid-1800s, mountain men were rough and tumble folk. Not only did they live without plumbing and electricity—as did everyone else during the period—but they also lived in remote cabins, often left completely to their own resources. If they wanted food they couldn't go to the farmer's market, they had to find it themselves.

They fished and hunted wild game, and if they had time and a bit of a green thumb they grew their own vegetable gardens, right there on the mountainside. They lived by their bravery and their wits. They also told a lot of stories. Much of what we have come to know about the legendary "Crow Killer" is folklore, since much of it was passed down as oral testimony before it was finally recorded in written form. But make no mistake, the life that this rugged mountain man led was an authentic one.

Unlike Paul Bunyan—John Jeremiah Johnson, A.K.A. the Crow Killer, was a real person. He began life fairly far removed from the mountains, on the East Coast. He was born in Pattenburg, New Jersey, as John Jeremiah Garrison. The name "Johnson" is actually an alias that he adopted later on after getting into some trouble during the Mexican-American war. He had gotten into a fight with one of his own commanders and then went AWOL.

Back in those days, it was much harder to catch up with a deserter, but John apparently decided a name change was necessary, just to make sure his previous handlers in the U.S. military weren't able to track him down. Under the name of "John Johnson", he started a new life in the rugged frontier countryside of Montana. Here he tried his luck at gold prospecting, trapping, and become adept at chopping and selling wood for the local lumber industry.

It was at some point during his early days out on the frontier, that he met a beautiful young woman who was known as "The Swan" or simply "Swan." She was of Native American origin and was part of a tribal group known as the Flatheads. John Johnson shared his simple life with his new wife, and for a time both were quite happy. And soon she was expecting their child.

This pure and simple happiness would be shattered, however, one fateful day in 1847, when John Johnson returned home to find his home ransacked and his pregnant wife Swan was dead. Not only was she dead—she was horribly mutilated with her scalp cut clean off. It was this incident that would spark a fire of vengeance in John Johnson that would never be extinguished.

John Johnson First Sets Out On His Own

"I became a loner. I became a mountain man. A lot of those things are very good qualities and they help you do your work; help you be singular and keep the artistic integrity of your work intact—but they don't make it very easy to live your life."
-John Milius

Oral history tells us that John Johnson was around 20 years old when he first disembarked from a steamship on St. Louis and headed for the mountain country of Missouri. Even back then, St. Louis was a bustling town, full of both opportunity and plenty of mischiefs. And the wide-eyed newcomers disembarking from watercraft were often targets of conmen, crooks, and criminals looking for that mischief.

Just about as soon as John Johnson stepped onto dry land, he was intercepted by one of these very mischief-makers. He was minding his own business, carrying a "skin rucksack" that was casually "thrown over his shoulder" when a local miscreant actually tried to grab the sack and take off with it.

The ruffian certainly couldn't have known what John was actually carrying. He couldn't have known whether he was stealing a bag of riches or a big bundle of junk. But just like the modern-day porch pirate willing to risk picking up an Amazon package full of dog crap from someone's porch—this thief was apparently willing to take his chances.

One thing this troublemaker didn't count on, however, was that he was messing with a young man who knew how to fight. Already cut loose from the military for his aggression toward senior officers, John Johnson was not someone who was willing to back down to anyone. As soon as John felt the thief tug on his rucksack, he instinctively and immediately whirled around and swung his free hand down on the interloper, knocking him from his feet.

The thief, bloody and sore from his fall, jumped up and acted as if he was going to strike John Johnson for the rebuff. John wasn't the least bit phased. He had learned a long time ago it's far better to go on the attack than to remain on the defensive. Fully answering the challenge, he dropped his bag down at his feet. And now with both hands-free, he was more than ready to take on this ruffian. He looked the guy in the eye and asked a simple question, "Don't you like it?"

With full-on mock sarcasm, John was showing his fearlessness even while taunting the troublemaker. He was basically asking him, "Hey buddy—you just got knocked on your ass. Don't you like it? And would you like some more of where that came from?"

Besides his bold words which indicated his fearless nature, something in John's eyes also instantly reaffirmed that he was not someone to be messed with. And after a moment, the thief realized he was no match for John Johnson. As such, he suddenly did an about-face and took off running in the other direction, trying to get as far away from John Johnson as he could.

With a few meager worldly possessions, as well as his own pride still fully intact, John tossed the bag back over his shoulder and went into town. It was here that he met a man described simply as an *old trader*—frontier-speak for a real wise guy—who knew the ins and outs of the community. That old trader was a man named "Joe Robidoux" who ran a local general store.

He had all of the basic items everyone needed, plus all of the town gossip and innuendo that anyone could ever want to hear. John began a simple enough conversation with the man, about his need for hunting rifles and traps. Joe obviously realized that this was a man looking to eke out an existence in the wild frontier country. Joe took a liking to John and invited him to take a load off and rest up in his store, while he prepared his provisions.

John ended up staying the night, sleeping on a pile of bags of grain for a makeshift bed. The storeowner had locked up after him—actually locking John *inside the store.* That way he wouldn't be able to steal, *or even leave*, without busting down the door himself. After a fitful sleep, John was greeted by the storeowner, shaking him awake early the next morning. As John wiped the sleep from his eyes, the old shopkeeper, Joe, invited him to have some breakfast with him.

It was over a meal of deer meat, corn bread, and coffee, that Joe really got to know John Johnson. A friendship was forged, and he decided he liked what he saw. The youth apparently had no family and didn't say much of anything about his past. But Joe, a keen reader of character, felt that he had found a kindred spirit.

Joe gladly supplied John with the best rifle his shop could offer and plenty of traps, and even a small horse to get around. These items weren't free of course, and John was no doubt using the last of his military pay to purchase them. But he was ready to go all-in, hoping that these supplies would be the starting point of a new life in the mountains. With his supplies in order, all that was left was to be pointed in the right direction.

For this, he sought to borrow some of Joe's great knowledge of the frontier country. Consulting with the old trader, John asked him where he could find the most abundant grounds for trapping wild varmints. Varmints whose hides he could skin and then sell for profit.

It's said that Joe, chomping on a piece of tobacco, thought about it for a moment, before he suddenly waved his hand westward and remarked, "There's good trapping out yonder on the Big Blue!" Led in what he thought was the right direction, John gave his most sincere thanks, said goodbye, and headed for the mountains.

In the Big Blue Country

"So, if you cannot understand that there is something in man which responds to the challenge of this mountain and goes out to meet it, that the struggle is the struggle of life itself—upward and forever upward. Then you won't see why we go. What we get from this adventure is just sheer joy. And joy is, after all, the end of life. We do not live to eat and make money. We eat and make money to be able to enjoy life. That is what life means and what life is for."
-George Leigh Mallory

John Johnson was in the thick of the wilderness laying out traps in the Big Blue Country. He thought that he was all alone—with no one around for miles. But just as his back was turned and he was getting one of his traps ready, he was stunned to hear a loud booming voice right behind him. He heard someone shout out something along the lines of "Your back makes a good target!"

Johnson slowly turned around to see a six-foot-tall mountain man, with long scraggly hair hanging over his shoulders. The man had a rifle pointed at him, but held it low enough to suggest that the interloper didn't mean so much aggression, but was rather exercising an abundance of caution. A quality that Johnson would soon learn was of the utmost importance. You had to be cautious out in the frontier after all, where it was essentially every man for himself.

The older man inquired with Johnson in a friendly enough manner, "What are you doing here, son?" It was then that John informed the man that he was told that the area was good for trapping. Upon hearing this the mountain man erupted in laughter, before informing John Johnson, that the place had already been "trapped out" a long time ago. According to this grizzled mountain man who introduced himself as John Hatcher, trappers had already hunted all of the valuable animals to virtual extinction long ago. And he was wasting his time in this area.

The man then disdainfully kicked John Johnson's trap aside and advised, "Come along with me, lad. But leave these things here. Where we're going, we make our own traps." Old John Hatcher then took a look at John Johnson's horse and after checking out the beast's hooves as well as inspecting its teeth (remember that expression doesn't look like a gift horse in the mouth?) he decided it was a good animal.

Even though Hatcher felt that Johnson had been bamboozled by the shopkeeper when he was told that the Big Blue was good for trapping, he couldn't help but admire the horse that he had sold Johnson. Hatcher is said to have remarked, "Wonders come and wonders go. Now—how come old Joe sold you a sound and fiery horse such as this?" Hatcher then led Johnson to his camp and the two ate some deer and further discussed their plans.

It was then that Hatcher informed the young trapper of a new way to make money. He showed him scalps he claimed to have retrieved from skirmishes with Native American tribesmen in the region. Hatcher told

Johnson that there was a huge market for these grisly trophies in England. Apparently, English aristocrats who would never dare set foot into the wilds of the frontier country loved to hang such grisly souvenirs from the fireplaces of their mansions back in London.

Johnson was shocked at what he heard. Perhaps he even began to have some misgivings about the stranger, but by now it was too late. For he had traveled so far with him, into territory he was completely unfamiliar with, he was now totally dependent on his newfound friend to be his guide. Cutting his losses and rolling the dice, Johnson ended up following Hatcher up into the "Unitah country" even deeper into the mountains, where John Hatcher promised the pickings (whether human or animal) were much more plentiful.

Some of this prospective human prey turned the tables on these would-be predators however, when shortly into their trek they were ambushed by a band of Arapahos. Arrows rained down on them in short order, and Johnson himself was hit in the shoulder with one of the arrow heads. Nevertheless, even with an arrow sticking out of him like the needle of a cactus, he managed to raise up his rifle and kill the man who had launched it.

Hatcher in the meantime began firing off his weapon with lightning speed, quickly killing two others, and sending the rest quite literally running for the hills. It was at that moment that Johnson realized just how valuable Hatcher was, as an experienced man of the mountains. Without his help, he no doubt would have been killed. Hatcher even proved his rudimentary medical skills. He took the "bowie knife" he carried and expertly cut out the arrow that was lodged in Johnson's shoulder.

This most certainly wasn't the first time that the grey-haired mountain man had to do such a thing. John Johnson couldn't help but be impressed. Hatcher for his part was also impressed with his newfound companion. For he could see that Johnson was one accustomed to dealing with pain. Johnson didn't make so much as a sound when Hatcher pulled the arrow out. Hatcher is said to have exclaimed, "Haven't you got no feelings? That [arrow] was deep!" But Johnson stoically soldiered on.

Before leaving their camp, Hatcher demonstrated the brutal technique of scalping for him. He went right up to one of the assailants that had been shot and prepared to scalp him. It was the keen eyes of Johnson, however, which noticed that this adversary was not quite dead. "[He's] still living!" Johnson shouted. Hatcher with the knife in hand then stabbed their opponent in the heart to make sure that he would not be among the living for much longer.

Hatcher then yanked the knife out of the man's chest and proceeded to scalp him. He carefully, and painstakingly showed John Johnson how to slice a "quick circle" of scalp off the head. He then roughly yanked on the man's hair (what Hatcher called the "topknot") in order to pull the scalp right off of his head. Hatcher then spun the freed scalp around in his hand to allow all of the excess blood and grime to come off in a swirl of spraying biological debris. Old John Hatcher then hung the scalp from a loop in his own belt.

With his grisly demonstration complete, he bid his new pupil John Johnson to try his luck on the other felled opponent, lying nearby. Without hesitation, Johnson carefully cut off the man's scalp in the same manner that he had been shown.

Hatcher was impressed at Johnson's quick study, and praised him, "You are better [suited] for this work than any man I ever saw." Johnson then carefully placed the scalp into his own belt. With their grisly trophies on hand, the two mountain men rode off together into the sunset.

Back at Hatcher's Old Homestead

"The mountains have rules. They are harsh rules, but they are there, and if you keep to them, you are safe. A mountain is not like men. A mountain is sincere. The weapons to conquer it exist inside you, inside your soul."
-Walter Bonatti

After their encounter with the Arapaho, Johnson, and Hatcher made their way back to Hatcher's own homestead. It was quite a journey to get there, and according to some accounts, Johnson even singlehandedly killed a bear on the way. The bear is said to have caught them off guard. Hatcher managed to shoot and wound the bear, before climbing up a tree to escape its grasp. This left Johnson alone with an enraged, wounded bear charging at him.

Johnson is said to have taken out his knife, and battling the animal on sheer instinct, ducked just as the beast swept at him with its claws. It was just as he was ducking down, that he plunged his knife into the animal's chest. The bear was hurt bad enough to fall back, giving Johnson time to run up the same tree that Hatcher had climbed into. Now they just had to wait for the beast to die and they would be on their way. And that's apparently what they did.

Since a lot of these testimonies are based on oral legends passed down, it's hard to know what's really true and what's not. This tale certainly isn't out of the realm of possibility. There are people that have successfully fought off bears. There was a man not too long ago who made the news by fending off a bear simply by giving it a good punch in the face. So, the story is at least feasible.

It was after their arduous trek that they found themselves at Hatcher's old homestead. Hatcher didn't live alone; it's said that he had taken up with two Native American women who shared a home and hearth with him. And Hatcher was apparently not too shy about sharing one of his girlfriends with Johnson. Or as the story goes, he "offered Johnson one of his women for the winter."

The narrative doesn't get too detailed about what this would have entailed, whether the woman would have worked for Johnson as a helper or something more. But Johnson quickly dismissed the offer, insisting that he was able to look after himself just fine. As they waited out the winter in the meantime, Hatcher continued to regale his newfound buddy Johnson, with tales of time gone by.

Johnson also had other guests arrive at whom Johnson was introduced, such as another fellow frontiersman by the name of Chris Lapp, or as he was otherwise known—*Bear Claw.* It was Bear Claw who would often keep Johnson company and help him find animals to trap when Johnson was away on official business, getting supplies or selling furs (and possibly scalps?) at nearby forts. Johnson in the meantime, quickly learned why Chris Lap was called "Bear Claw."

He enjoyed trapping bears and cutting off their claws, which he then turned into necklaces that he wore with pride. He was himself a silver-haired mountain man, but he still had something of the artistic streak inside him, the way he perfected his finely crafted bear claw necklaces. Johnson in the meantime, still in his early 20s, had reached the height of his physical powers. He was a big, strong, strapping young man at six foot two and 240 pounds. He became respected as a fighter, known to be able to take on "any two men" at the same time.

According to one story, in fact, he got into an argument with a local Sioux trader and ended up taking on five people at one time. It's said that he was more than ready to tear all of them limb from limb. How much of this is true and how much is a sheer exaggeration is hard to know—but Johnson was most certainly a tough character regardless. So much so, that he was made a part of the so-called "camp police" a group of vigilantes in the mountain community made up of local trappers and even some Native Americans, who sought to keep the peace between temperamental locals.

If there was ever a problem in the community, and an argument got out of hand, John Johnson could be relied upon to break up the squabble. According to some accounts, however, Johnson didn't always simply bring peace so much as eradicate the troublemakers.

One account speaks of how he intervened when two warriors from rival tribes were threatening each other with knives. As the two men circled around each other, Johnson allegedly walked right up, grabbed both by the head with each of his strong hands, and viciously slammed their heads together. Both of these men fell down and did not get up again.

Did Johnson really keep the peace by killing those who dared to disrupt it? If true, he was clearly more than ready to engage in violence even before his long-standing vendetta against the Crow tribe began.

Crazy Woman and Tragic Mountain Magic

"The desire for magic cannot be eradicated. Even the most supposedly rational people attempt to practice magic in love and war. We simultaneously possess the most primitive of brain stems and the most sophisticated of cortices. The imperatives of each coexist uneasily."
-Erica Jong

By the summer of 1846, Johnson had already established his own successful base of operations in Montana. Despite any previous misgivings, he found suitable animals to trap and when the trapping season was "lean" he found extra work by cutting up wood and selling it down river to local steamboat captains who made use of the firewood on their ships. It was during that same fateful, productive summer, however, that Johnson came face to face with a horrible sight.

He stumbled upon a family that had just been massacred by a local tribal group. There was one survivor—the wife and mother of three children. She had followed her husband John Morgan out west in the hopes of starting a new life. They had stopped in the middle of their journey to take a rest when Mr. Morgan turned up missing after taking their oxen to a nearby field to graze. Mrs. Morgan sent her two boys to look for them—but they too failed to return.

She then sent her daughter to look around. It was shortly after her daughter attempted to locate her brothers and father, that Mrs. Morgan heard an ear-piercing scream. It was her daughter's own blood-curdling howls that filled the air. It sounded as if she were under attack. Full of adrenaline, Mrs. Morgan immediately went into action. She grabbed an ax and without hesitation ran toward the sound of her daughter's cries. She then came upon a horrible sight.

Her husband was tied to a stake, his scalp cut clean off, and apparently just barely still alive. Her two boys were laying on the ground dead, also scalped. And her daughter was on the ground with her clothes ripped off, in the process of being raped by a member of the Blackfoot tribe. Several other Blackfoot fighters also stood nearby. In a desperate frenzy of rage, Mrs. Morgan charged at the attackers.

They were so stunned, that they failed to even respond in time, as she hacked into them. It's said that she actually managed to kill four of them before the rest fled. The surviving Blackfoot warriors took the dying John Morgan with them, before bolting off on their horses.

Now, it must be said that this story certainly seems a little hard to believe. The fact that Mrs. Morgan allegedly killed four of the warriors, thereby avenging the four lives (her husband, two sons, and daughter) that they took—seems just a little too neat and perfect to be entirely real. Four for four. Four died—so four were killed. Poetic justice at its best, right?

Or perhaps it just sounded good to the storyteller who made up the tall tale? We can't know for certain. But it certainly seems that in many of these tales that come from oral accounts you do find what seems to be this kind of superficial embellishment worked into the overall narrative of events.

According to this account, John Johnson came on the scene in the immediate aftermath of this bloodbath. It's said that the daughter had since died of her injuries, and the mother was in the process of attempting to bury her slain children upon his arrival. She also managed to bury the scalp of her husband that the warriors had dropped when they fled. Without hesitation, John Johnson rushed over and helped the distraught woman, with this terrible task.

And as an extra flourish, the enraged mother supposedly drove a stake in front of each of the four graves and topped each stake with the head of one of the four warriors she had killed. More poetic justice, maybe? These grisly posts would stand as a testament to the horrors that had occurred and as a warning to others.

Johnson unsure of what else to do to help, took some time to build a ramshackle log cabin for Mrs. Morgan right on the spot. Once this task was complete, he then handed her a rifle to defend herself and headed off to Hatcher's homestead.

The narrative becomes a bit jumbled and hard to follow at this point, but it's said that Hatcher had decided to go out west to California and after sending his two girlfriends back to their "people, the Cheyenne, with plenty of supplies" he invited Johnson to take over as the man of his homestead.

John Johnson in the meantime later received word of how Mrs. Morgan was faring. Others in the community apparently checked in on her and on several occasions had attempted to get her to move out to a safer, more established community. But Mrs. Morgan insisted she wanted to stay by the graves of her family members. Instead, she essentially became a self-reliant mountain woman. Actually, the nickname the gun-toting widow was given was—"Crazy Woman".

She was known to be crazed with grief and more than ready to blow away anyone who gave her a hard time. Most poignant of all, it was said that every night around the time that her family was attacked she would break down into the most piteous howls and sobs, which could be heard from miles around.

Local gossips even went so far as to speak of curses, magic, witchcraft, and enchantment as it pertained to Crazy Woman's ramshackle homestead. The local tribes all feared her and viewed her as a powerful medicine woman of the mountains. But those who actually took the time to learn about her sad and entirely tragic story—knew the truth.

John Jonson in the meantime had heard that Crazy Woman's husband had actually survived and escaped from his captors. Johnson didn't go and share this news with Crazy Woman, because that simply wasn't how mountain men conducted themselves. In the typical mountain man mentality, Johnson figured that if Mr. Morgan did not wish to seek out his wife, he had his own reasons. Perhaps he was too sad and traumatized—maybe he simply wanted to forget.

Most might criticize the man for such a thing—but for Johnson, it was simply none of his business. It was not anything for him to become involved in. So, he didn't mention it. Johnson much preferred stoic silence to stir up any raw emotion and (at least what he viewed to be) unnecessary drama. As far as he was concerned, such things simply went with the territory, for those who chose to make their living in the wilds of the mountains.

The Mountain Man and the Swan

"For beauty with sorrow is a burden hard to be borne. The evening light on the foam, and the swans, there—that music, remote, forlorn."
-Walter de la Mare

In early 1847, as soon as the first glimmers of Springtime were on the horizon, John Johnson loaded up all of the furs he had accumulated that winter from trapping and readied them for sale. He set off on his journey to sell his wares, but Johnson ended up making a slight detour. By May he found himself at the camp of a local Flathead tribe. He had become acquainted previously with the tribal leader, and upon being invited to pay them a visit, he didn't hesitate to join them.

Johnson, as much as he was known to seek vengeance on warriors whom he felt had crossed him or were a threat, was equally open to friendship with those whom he understood to be clear allies. And the relationship he had with this Flathead tribe was clearly a mutually benevolent one. He traded goods with the tribe, and on this particular occasion, he sat down to eat a great feast with them.

It was at some point during the feasting and festivities that a proposal was made for Johnson to take the chief's daughter as a bride. It remains unclear if it was Johnson or the chief who made this suggestion. But apparently, the chief was in full agreement with the proposal, and after receiving gifts of "one rifle, two knives, and a supply of salt and sugar" Johnson was presented with the chief's daughter to take as his own wife.

She was considered quite delicate and beautiful in appearance, and it was due to her graceful nature that she had been dubbed "The Swan." Or simply "Swan" for short. As much as we might take offense to a man seemingly "selling" his daughter to be married to another man, this was apparently quite common in many tribal groups. If Swan was not bartered off in this fashion to Johnson, she would have been bartered off to someone else in a similar way.

At any rate, it's said that Swan took a liking to Johnson and saw him as an honest man and potentially as a good provider. As such, she was pleased to go with him, rather than being bartered off like some chess piece to some rival tribe, in which her fate might be much more uncertain.

Johnson for his part was quite happy to have someone help him with chores around his homestead. He was able to happily smoke and chew tobacco while the Swan kept the fire warm, and otherwise took care of the domestic aspects of frontier life. Johnson also put a lot of trust in his new wife, giving her a gun of her own and teaching her how to make use of it.

He also learned quite a bit from her as well. She shared with him local tribal customs, such as how to make moccasins. The sure-footed moccasin would indeed be of great aid to Johnson in his later endeavors since it would allow him to easily sneak up on both human and animal prey alike. But perhaps most importantly, the Swan taught him to eventually become quite fluent in the Flathead language.

Johnson could only spend a few months with his bride, however, before he had to leave her behind that winter. He had business to take care of in the bustling fur trade. He made sure that she was well provisioned, however, with plenty of food and supplies and promised he would be back as soon as possible. Little did Johnson know—he wasn't just leaving one family member behind—but two. The Swan was already pregnant with his child.

In her husband's absence, the Swan spent her days quietly taking care of the homestead. She would hunt small animals with the gun Johnson had given her. Cook her meals, and mend moccasins by the fire. She was engaged in the latter when a group of Crow warriors snuck up on her. It seems that they were most likely spying on this particular homestead for some time. And once they realized that this woman was all by herself, they struck.

Swan had little chance of defending herself as the tomahawk came crashing down on her from behind. She was hit in the neck and knocked to the ground. The warrior then pounced on top of her, and quickly cut her scalp from her head. The shouting warriors then ransacked the whole cabin, stealing everything inside and out that they could, including a small horse that Johnson had given to Swan.

They then rode off, leaving death and destruction in their wake. Johnson returned to this terrible sight several weeks later. His wife had been left to rot and decay right out in the open. And upon reaching the homestead, Johnson was greeted by his wife's glaring skeleton, which was in the process of being picked at by a vulture.

Johnson despite his immense grief, immediately began to investigate what was essentially a crime scene. Here the mountain man turned detective and found what he believed to be the telltale sign that the assailants had been members of the Crow tribe. He found a long eagle feather—the signature calling card of the Crow warrior. He then made an ominous pledge. He committed himself to waging what was essentially a one-man war against the entire Crow nation.

The Vendetta Begins

*"I have always supported measures and principles—
and not men."
- Davy Crockett*

The first signs that something terrible was lurking in the mountains, hunting and picking off Crow warriors at will, came to the surface sometime in 1848. Members of the Crow tribe were turning up dead apparently at random. These deaths did not seem to be the results of a struggle or robbery—but rather, entirely haphazard killings. And it was noted that it was only members of the Crow tribe that were being hunted down in these slayings.

Yet as random as these slayings were, they had certain repeating hallmarks. All of the dead men had been scalped and their livers had been removed. In the world of criminology today, such a thing would immediately be identified as the work of a serial killer, leaving behind their own signature calling cards. Yes, long before the term "serial killer" was ever even in use—the exact kind of behavior was on display.

Someone was killing—and they were killing to send a clear and deliberate message to everyone else—that they had a beef with the Crows. Local talk then began to swirl around John Johnson.

And in a short time, it became widely believed that he was killing Crow warriors out of revenge for what had happened to his wife. It was at this point, that he was dubbed the "Crow Killer."

The wild mountain frontier certainly had its share of characters. There were plenty of wild stories about "Crazy Woman", "Bear Claw" and the like—but now the locals had an even more formidable semi-mythical figure in the form of the "Crow Killer". Even worse, in relation to rumors that Johnson was removing the livers of his enemies to feast upon them, he was also sometimes referred to as "Liver-Eating Johnson."

As the year progressed into 1849, miners began to hit it big in the California Gold Rush. Wayward travelers through the mountains on their way to California were filled with wild tales of the Crow Killer. They then passed these stories on, all the way to the west coast. This was one of the primary means by which this incredible story began to gain tremendous traction early on.

The story was so widespread, that at one point it's said that folks would even joke about it with their kids. Many parents, when having trouble getting their children to behave, would tell their kids that if they weren't careful, they would, "get Liver-Eating Johnson after you!"

Even more dramatic, were the real-life encounters of strangers with the guy who had been dubbed the "Crow Killer." And when he came to trading posts, those who were unprepared for the sight would shudder in the knowledge of what this man might have done. It was later said by locals, that when the grim figure of the Crow Killer passed them by, they felt as if the Grim Reaper of Death himself had just crossed their path.

Still, he had plenty of fine furs—as well as scalps—to swap. And he always came away from the trading post with plenty of bullets, gunpowder, salt, and coffee to take back with him. Long after the Crow Killer had left, some of the braver souls are said to have cracked jokes about how Johnson must need the salt to spice up all of those livers he was eating.

But we're getting ahead of ourselves. Now that we understand the notoriety that had developed—how did this one-man war against the Crows begin? Well, it seems that shortly after his wife's death, John Johnson was able to track down not just a random Crow warrior—but her actual killers.

The Crows had commonly traded with the Flathead tribe from whence Swan came, and it was apparent through John Johnson's contacts with the Flathead people that he picked up enough intelligence to locate the whereabouts of her killers.

He followed them right to a trading post where Crow and Flathead would exchange their wares. Among them, he no doubt saw stolen goods from his own home being traded off. The Flathead people, of course, can't be blamed for this. They certainly had no way of knowing they were being given stolen property. They just accepted whatever the Crows traded them and moved on.

John Johnson, the Crow Killer himself, in the meantime, had followed the whole contingent of warriors, and remained hidden at a distance, while the trading went down. He had to bide his time. John Johnson knew full well he couldn't suddenly charge the group and challenge them in open combat. Despite his years of taking on bears and fighting two men at once, even he wasn't ferocious enough to take on a whole gang of warriors.

Instead, he continued to follow the group, after they left the trading post, and waited for the perfect moment to strike. He was so careful not to be detected, that he improvised some moccasin-styled footgear for his horse. He actually wrapped horsehide around the hooves of the animal, in order to both muffle the sound of the hoofbeats, as well as eliminate any hoofprints.

He managed to trail them all the way to their base camp a short distance away near a river, in a spot referred to as the "forks of the Beaverhead." Getting off his horse, he hid in a thicket and continued to observe the encampment from afar. In the distance, he could see the flicker of their fire, and he was also able to make out two shapes—two guards keeping watch as the others slept.

One was tending the fire and the other was constantly pacing about, lest anyone approach them unaware. Johnson knew that it was these two guards that he would have to subdue first. Even from a distance, his eagle eyes were able to make out a high stack of buffalo hide which the Crow were likely hauling with them to trade.

As he mentally mapped out his plan, the buffalo hide appeared to be a good place to hide (no pun intended) behind, before he made his first strike. With this plan in mind, Johnson took a breath and made his approach. He very slowly crept toward the camp, making sure not to make a sound. He was then able to duck right behind the mountain of buffalo hide.

Johnson lay in wait behind the hide, and as soon as the pacing guard walked by, he picked up a huge rock and threw it at the guard's head with all of his might. The rock hit home and knocked the guard out cold. The fact that this man could toss a rock and hit the guard in just the right place, with just enough pressure to knock him out, is either the product of a tall tale (maybe it didn't happen like that at all!) or a testament to a guy who was highly skilled when it came to utilizing both his sheer strength, as well as his coordination.

Whatever the case may be, the general narrative holds that the Crow Killer was able to knock down this first Crow guard without any problems. Johnson then quickly grabbed up the guard and dragged him back to the thicket. Then Johnson executed the second part of his plan, he rushed over to where the Crow's horses were and set them loose.

As soon as he did, he let out a Crow-style war-*whoop!* The sound of horses as well as the battle cry, caused the whole camp to wake up in chaos. This chaos was exactly what the Crow Killer was looking to create. Under the cover of all of this drama, Johnson then went back to the unconscious Crow warrior and scalped him.

He observed that the man reflexively shook after doing so, indicating that he was indeed still alive. Johnson then took the time to slit the Crow man's throat. Looking down at the man's belt, he noticed a scalp with long black hair hanging from it. Johnson is said to have instinctively recognized the hair as having belonged to his wife, the Swan. In a moment of stunning clarity, he realized that he had just slain the very man who had killed his wife.

And the Vendetta Continues...

"Inside of me, there are two dogs. One is mean and evil and the other is good and they fight each other all the time. When asked which one wins, I answer—the one I feed the most."
-Chief, Sitting Bull

After killing his first Crow, the Crow Killer knew that soon he would have the wrath of the whole Crow Nation coming down upon him. As such, he didn't stay in the same place for long. Instead, he headed over to the friendly territory of his Flathead allies. He rode as fast as he could, on barely any sleep, straight to the Flathead camp. It's said that he rode so fast in fact, that he wore his animal down completely. And by the time they stopped in Flathead territory and Johnson dismounted, the animal faltered and fell—collapsing at Johnson's feet.

Johnson ended up having to pull out his gun to put the animal down. Again, we can't be certain how many of these details are true or sheer exaggerations. The idea that his horse was driven to its death and just so happened to collapse at his feet after he dismounted, smacks of romantic embellishments. Such details are great for storytelling since they add to the desperation of the moment. But the jury is still out on whether or not such an event really took place or not.

At any rate, it most likely was a dramatic scene when John Johnson stepped onto Flathead territory and greeted his friends and former in-laws. He was led to the main encampment by a couple of kids who were out "lizard hunting." Johnson's skills in the tribal language, taught to him by his late wife, no doubt helped him to navigate his way through these complex social situations.

Johnson found himself at the main encampment, in a large field, where several hundred horses had been parked, which the Flathead people were saving to trade with the locals. Here Johnson came upon two guards and was able to explain that he was a friend of the Chief. He was allowed entrance and subsequently given an audience with his former father-in-law.

The Chief saw Johnson and rose up to greet him, placing his hand on Johnson's chest, as was the custom of close relatives. The two men then sat down and the Chief had a pipe and tobacco brought for them to smoke. It was after they smoked in silence for a few minutes that Johnson began to speak to the Chief in his own tongue. It's said that the Chief was surprised and quite pleased to see that his son-in-law had learned the Flathead language well enough.

But what happened next only brought the Chief complete and utter sorrow. For John Johnson explained what had happened to the Swan, and showed the shocked Chief the scalp that he had retrieved. The Chief took the scalp and ran his fingers through the hair as he shook with grief, and acknowledged, "It is the Swan." Johnson explained that it was the Crows who had killed her and the Chief filled with rage at the mention immediately demanded that revenge be brought down on them all.

Johnson then informed him, that these Crows had recently been trading with the Flathead people and that they would likely soon be back. To this, the Chief shouted in defiance, "My warriors will be ready. We will trade death!"

The old man then thanked Johnson for getting vengeance for his daughter's killing and then assured him once again that his own fighters would get more revenge on the rest, should they dare return to Flathead territory. After this meeting, it's said that the Chief gifted his son-in-law with a new horse, and the fierce and determined Crow Killer rode out of the encampment.

Flathead warriors, in the meantime, left as an advance guard to monitor any movement on the part of the Crows. A couple hundred more Flathead fighters were placed around the entrance of the encampment ready to ambush the Crow warriors as soon as they showed their faces.

The next time Johnson returned to the Flathead encampment; he saw some 36 fresh scalps hanging in the Chief's lodgings. He learned that only 13 of their number had escaped. The Chief now considered his family to have been avenged. Yet, for the Crow Killer, his long vendetta against the Crows was just getting started.

Over the next several months, Johnson would continue killing Crow warriors at random; soon the Crows themselves had to accept the disturbing fact that they were being specifically targeted. They had heard rumors of a man who was avenging the slaying of his wife, but the continued killings seemed over the top.

The situation was confirmed however when a warrior was sent to conduct surveillance on the house in which the Swan was slain. The warrior spotted Johnson in the yard cradling the skull of his slain wife and came back to confirm that the wild mountain man called the Crow Killer was indeed the husband of a woman recently slain by the Crows. They now had to accept that they were all on the receiving end of a terrible vendetta.

And as the targeted attacks continued, even their tribal enemies began to take notice. Most of them found great sport in mocking the Crows whenever they encountered them at trading posts. In the world of first nations peoples, honor meant a lot. And the notion that one man was so thoroughly terrorizing a whole tribe was said to have been a source of great dishonor.

So much so, that the Crows were forced to hold a grand council so that they could openly discuss what to do about this crazed serial killer in their midst. The obvious answer would be to assemble a huge war party, overwhelm the man and kill him outright. They knew where he lived after all, and even this crazy mountain man would not be able to fend off a whole raiding party laying siege to his homestead.

But the whole situation had gotten to such a point, that such a seemingly easy solution was no longer on the table. The leadership of the Crow knew all too well, that if they sent hundreds of their best men to face off against one lone mountain man, they would become even further laughing stocks. Were these the mighty Crow warriors of old—reduced to having to send overwhelming odds against one man?

They realized that the only honorable way to get rid of the menace of the Crow Killer would be to send their best, most powerful warriors to engage him in single combat. They sought to have them sicked on the Crow Killer in waves, one after the other, hoping at the very least to wear him out so much that one of the fresh, solitary warriors sent to him, would finally be able to subdue him. Such tactics were not altogether fair, but it would be enough to at least save some precious face amongst their peers.

Their plan would fail miserably, however. And although Johnson would never reveal exactly how it all went down, he would eventually have 20 Crow warrior scalps to show that he managed to best 20 different Crow fighters in single combat—one after the other. Johnson in the meantime, in the midst of all of this, kept up contact with old friends such as Bear Claw, and also a character whose name comes down to us as "Del Gue."

It was in 1855, that Del Gue would later claim to have been on an expedition with the Crow Killer and bore witness to his Crow-killing technique firsthand. They were out in the open, sitting around a fire when Johnson suddenly stood up and backed away. He then ordered Del Gue to put out the fire. Del Gue did as instructed and the next thing he knew, Johnson was kicking a shadowy form whom he had sent—

courtesy of his moccasin-clad foot—flying in the other direction.

The stunned man was barely able to get to his feet before Johnson delivered another swift kick to his person and brought him down to the ground once again. Johnson then leaped upon the man and plunged his knife deep into his heart, killing him. Yet another Crow had been slain at Johnson's hands. This warrior had apparently been just one of the latest, trying to get the drop on the Crow Killer, but was entirely unable to do so.

Once the man was dead, Johnson then took his blade and quickly scalped his slain opponent. Despite his friend's protests of not wanting to see such a display, Johnson proceeded to cut open the man's torso and reached his own hand inside to remove the liver. Del Gue couldn't ever quite get the image of this out of his mind and would report this incident as absolute fact, several years later.

The Crow Killer Captured...
But Not for Long

"I wouldn't give a tinker's damn for a man who isn't sometimes afraid. Fear's the spice that makes it interesting to go ahead."
-Daniel Boone

As good as the Crow Killer was at detecting danger—and as vigilant as his senses were when it came to detecting that his enemies were near—sometime in early 1861 he would finally slip up and make some rather serious miscalculations. For it was around this time, that he was captured and taken prisoner while attempting to haul some bootlegged whiskey through the mountains.

He wasn't taken by his nemesis the Crow, however, but rather by a group of Blackfeet warriors. He had been passing for days through their territory and the sight of him and his pack animals loaded with booze was apparently a bit too much for them to resist. They decided to attack.

John Johnson didn't happen to notice the group of warriors who were quietly leering at him, from behind a pile of large boulders, beside the trail he traveled. And by the time a hail of arrows came down right on top of him, it was too late. For a split second, he considered raising his gun, but his enemies were well protected by the rock outcroppings that they were stationed behind.

Being out in the open as he was—a pure and simple target—for once in his life, the Crow Killer realized that he was simply outmatched and outgunned. He knew that if he lifted up his rifle to fire upon these assailants, it wouldn't have taken much for them to kill him right there on the spot—or at least this was the rationale that John Johnson gave later on, after the fact.

One can only wonder, however, how things might have shaped up, had he done something truly innovative, such as using one of his pack animals as a shield as he barreled over to the side of the road with both his guns blazing. At any rate, Johnson at the time did not think he had any way out of the trap he was caught in. As such, he did something he had never done in his life before.

He put down his weapon and put his hands up into the air as a gesture of surrender. Knowing that he would likely be killed and scalped—boggles the mind what John Johnson thought he could accomplish by surrendering, but nevertheless, he clearly believed that surrender was indeed in order. According to Johnson's later account, once his attackers realized that they could take him and his cargo without a fight, the leader of the group came out from the rocks to greet him.

It was then that apparently, this warrior realized who John Johnson was, and shouted, "The Killer of Crows has at last been taken!" Since the Blackfeet were a traditional rival of the Crow tribe, it was rather unclear how the Blackfeet would view Johnson and his previous exploits. Johnson supposedly took it all in stride, however, simply remarking stoically, "All things come to pass."

Johnson apparently recognized the tribal affiliation of the group, then sought to remind them, "I ain't no enemy of the Blackfoots." It was true that he wasn't an enemy of the Blackfoot tribe, but he wasn't exactly an ally either. His relationship with them was more or less neutral. But Johnson was friends with an ancestral enemy of the Blackfoot people—since he was still close to his former in-laws—the Flatheads.

And Johnson made a grave mistake by momentarily forgetting the antagonism that existed between these two tribes. For when the Blackfoot leader happened to ask him where he was taking the whiskey, he slipped up and replied, "To my friends the Flatheads."

This elicited an immediate response of contempt from the Blackfoot leader. After openly deriding the Flatheads, he indicated what he would do with Johnson—he would sell him to his mortal enemy the Crows. Johnson being handed over to the Crows, of course, would be a fate worse than death.

Nevertheless, John Johnson's goods were seized and he was then forced to walk on foot—he was led to the Blackfoot camp. The warriors in the meantime periodically jeered and beat their captive as he progressed on this grim, forced march. Upon his arrival at the Blackfeet camp, Johnson was tied up and unceremoniously dumped into a nearby teepee.

Here he was guarded by one lone warrior, while the rest of the bunch began to engage in a great celebration at Johnson's expense. He could hear the raucous singing and laughter as the other Blackfeet warriors drank their fill of the whiskey he had carried. Johnson then bided his time, as he watched his guard become increasingly distracted—and perhaps feeling more than a little left out—by the joyous celebration taking place in the camp. All the while, Johnson was pulling and tearing at his restraints whenever the guard wasn't looking.

Finally, the warrior was given some booze of his own. The strong drink must have distracted the young fighter even more. For when Johnson finally succeeded in breaking his restraints, the guard barely even seemed to register what was happening—he was slow to respond, and Johnson quickly got the drop on him, and with what was now his signature move—he kicked the brave, knocking him to the ground.

Johnson then delivered a vicious hammering blow to the young man's head, rendering him entirely unresponsive on the floor of the teepee. Johnson, wasting no time, grabbed the knife that the young warrior carried and took it for his own. He had to make his escape, but not before engaging in his ultimate signature act. He quickly sliced off the warrior's scalp and placed it in his belt.

It remains unclear if this Blackfoot fighter was still alive at the time when the Crow Killer scalped him. If he was, this previously whiskey-swilling fighter most certainly must have woken up with a terrible hangover. But according to Johnson's account, even worse was in store for this former guard of the Crow Killer. Because as terrible as it sounds, Johnson supposedly took his blade and cut deep into the unconscious man's leg, right through the top of his thigh, before ranking the man's leg right off. Why would he do such a horrible thing?

Well, apparently since Johnson knew that he had a long journey ahead of him, and livers alone wouldn't be enough to sustain him, he was ready to take the man's leg with him so he could cannibalize it later. Yes, the Crow Killer was apparently already thinking ahead to his next meal. It's shocking and incredibly hard to believe—but this man was apparently capable of anything.

Johnson is said to have then slipped out of the teepee, and under the cover of darkness, with a chopped-off leg slung over his shoulder, he made his way out of the Blackfoot camp. He had escaped, but now he had to figure out what to do next. Bereft of his horse he would have to walk to either his homestead, which at this point was a couple of hundred miles behind him or to the Flathead camp which was even further away.

Even worse, it had begun to snow, and since the Blackfoot warriors had robbed him of his coat, he very much risked getting pneumonia, while he was stranded out in the elements. Not knowing what else to do, he continued to put one foot in front of the other (even as he literally carried the leg and foot of a Blackfeet warrior slung over his shoulder!).

He did the best he could, traveling by day and then curling up in caves or behind rock outcroppings in the freezing cold of night. He did whatever he could to reserve warmth so that he didn't freeze to death. He didn't dare light a fire, however, until he had put several days between himself and the Blackfoot camp. Once he was able to do so, he lit up a fiery blaze and began cutting flesh from the leg he carried, in order to cook himself up a hearty meal of cannibalized meat.

The leg was apparently still fairly fresh since the cold weather prevented it from spoiling. So yes, just imagine this madman in a cave in front of a fire, gnawing on a former enemy's leg bone for sustenance. Even if this story is complete fiction—this tale of John Johnson gnawing on the leg bone of a former foe was repeated verbatim for several years. Even if it didn't happen, the fact that it was repeated with such relish, gives one an idea of the kind of dark humor that was so common among mountain folk on the frontier.

According to some later accounts of John Johnson, it was after he escaped from the Blackfoot tribe that he embarked on a renewed quest of revenge—not against his old nemesis the Crow, but against the Blackfoot themselves. Aiding him in this venture were several of his mountain men buddies. It's said that they assembled a whole posse to pursue these enemies of John Jeremiah Johnson.

These men were skilled hunters used to tracking wild game, and they used these very skills to track down the Blackfoot encampment. Once they discovered where the Blackfoot had set up their tents, they descended upon the warriors with complete abandon. The Blackfoot fighters apparently taken completely unaware, didn't know what hit them as this band of grizzly grey mountain men descended upon them.

In the bloodbath that ensued, it's said that the entire encampment soon "resembled a slaughterhouse." The mountain men apparently emerged with several scalps in their possession, and John Johnson himself came out of it with the entire decapitated head of the Blackfoot leader in his hand. This he put on a stake that was driven into the ground in front of the encampment. In full, terrible medieval style, this grisly signpost was apparently meant to serve as a warning for anyone else who would dare mess with the Crow Killer.

The Last Crow and the Last Batch of Biscuits for the Road

"It was because of my great interest in the West, and my belief that its development would be assisted by the interest I could awaken in others—that I decided to bring the West to the East through the medium of the Wild West Show."
-Buffalo Bill

As mentioned earlier in this book, after the Crow council had convened to figure out how to deal with the Crow Killer, they determined to send Crow warriors after him one by one. According to official Crow Killer lore, this group of killers originally numbered 20. At this point in the Crow Killer saga, all but one of this original 20 had been killed.

The Crow Killer is said to have encountered this last and final Crow adversary, in the most mundane of ways. He was at home baking biscuits. Besides being a one-man war machine, the Crow Killer was apparently also quite well known for his skills as a baker. And with just some flour, some bear grease, and a few other sparse ingredients, he was known to whip up some rather tasty biscuits.

He was baking a whole batch of them on the fateful day of this last encounter, planning to stow them in his pack for food on his next journey abroad. He had just finished baking the biscuits and had left them on top of the stove when he went out to wash the pan that he had just baked them in. This was of course, long before running water, so the mountain man did what came naturally, he went to a nearby creek and began scrubbing the pan with an old rag and creek water.

It was while he was busy with this task over at the nearby creek that he sensed some movement back at the old homestead. He looked over and to his shock, he saw a large Crow warrior in his kitchen stuffing his face with biscuits. The biscuits were indeed irresistible, and this intruder seems to have taken quite a liking to them. The warrior sent to kill John Johnson was so distracted by the flour-based foodstuffs in fact, that he did not notice John walk right up behind him.

As was his typical routine, John gave the Crow warrior a swift kick and sent him flying. John then leaped upon his foe and stabbed him right in the heart. Johnson had just scalped the man when his buddy Del Gue happened to stop by. It was apparently Del Gue's arrival that prevented the Crow Killer from ripping out the man's liver, as was his typical routine.

He decided to spare his friend Del the sight. Although he did spend some time joking with him about how "mighty tasty" liver and biscuits would have been. It was apparently his visitor Del Gue who reminded him that this was the 20th Crow that he had killed. The fact that this Crow had been tracking him for so long filled Johnson with a surprising degree of admiration. Perhaps even a little pity.

He realized that this warrior had been tracking him away from home and hearth for several years. This guy due to his pledge to not rest until the Crow Killer was slain, had spent many seasons in hardship, in the cold, and without proper food. The Crow Killer decided that the dedication this warrior had displayed, had most certainly earned him the biscuits he had eaten.

At any rate, the Crow Killer still had quite a journey ahead of him the next day. And as intriguing as such things were to contemplate, he couldn't waste time dwelling on them. So, with a shrug of his massive shoulders, he told his friend, "I'll be making more biscuits tomorrow."

Now, as anyone can see, these stories have more than a little twinge of old folksy witticisms. As mentioned earlier, the narrative as presented is often just way too neat and tidy in its telling, to seem believable. John Johnson comes off as some kind of 19th-century superhero (or maybe supervillain) who has a down pat routine.

Over and over again, we hear the story of how he kicks his opponent, knocks them down, stabs them, scalps them, and then eats their liver (maybe even with a side of biscuits). It makes you wonder if someone around a campfire developed this formulaic narrative about a wild frontiersman and then used it as a template to create folksy, dark humor-filled stories set in the trappings of the kind of hard, rustic life that frontier people would be familiar with.

Even the last parting refrain of the story, where Johnson is said to have summed up the days' horrific events by simply stating, "I'll be making more biscuits tomorrow" seems like a comic invention of some wily mountain man's dry, dark humor. A grimly poetic parting shot of the relentlessness of life in the mountains. Yes, he killed someone—but right in line with the attitude of the rugged rustic—life goes on, and there were still biscuits that needed to be made regardless.

The narrative is just a bit too neat and tidy, the way it is put together—to seem entirely believable. In many ways, it seems more like a dark, frontier version of a Grimm's fairy tale, than an account of real life. But then again you never know. As much as there seems to be some embellishment in these tales told among mountain men—the truth is indeed sometimes stranger than fiction.

And several years later, another odd and entirely strange tale involving Johnson and a pan of biscuits emerged. Supposedly in 1871, Johnson took out a whole band of Blackfoot warriors who were after him, simply by tricking them into eating a panful of biscuits that he had personally poisoned with a dose of strychnine.

As the story goes, John Johnson had met up with some fellow mountain men at Fort McPherson in Nebraska in the summer of 1871. This was apparently the group's pre-rendezvous point before they launched a planned expedition into the nearby Big Horn Mountains, to engage in extensive hunting and trapping.

According to this account, another rather famous individual of the frontier made their presence known at this gathering. For it's claimed that none other than Buffalo Bill was hanging out at Fort McPherson at the time. Buffalo Bill was apparently recruiting real-life wild men of the frontier to work as "actors" for a live-action production that he was going to take to theatre venues out east.

Johnson apparently had nothing but "contempt" for the promoter whom he essentially viewed as a fake cowboy, and sought to avoid him at all cost. At one point one of his buddies jokingly asked him to recruit Bill, at which Johnson allegedly retorted, "Might get his britches dirty in them Big Horns!"

He apparently figured that the nicely dressed Buffalo Bill wouldn't want to get down and dirty with them in the true wilderness of the mountain country. Nevertheless, the mountain man got together their posse and headed off to the Big Horn Mountains as planned. The trek there was uneventful though the danger was always a possibility since the path they traveled on led them over Sioux claimed territory in the Black Hills.

The men made it to their destination without a problem and set up shop. They then spent the rest of their time in what Johnson termed a "real fur pocket" and trapped and hunted the plentiful game therein. On one occasion, however, they returned to camp to find it ransacked. Their horses were gone, as well as recently collected fur pelts. It was also noted that a whole pan of biscuits had been consumed by the intruders.

It was this incident that prompted Johnson to deduce that the culprits were likely from the Blackfoot tribe. In order to justify his assumption, Johnson stated that they were the "Biggest biscuit eaters in the world." He made the statement as if the love for biscuits was some obvious, identifying clue.

John Johnson then came up with a dastardly scheme to get back at those who had robbed them. He made up a fresh batch of biscuits but was sure to mix a special ingredient in with the flour. As mentioned earlier, he did the unthinkable—he put a hearty dose of strychnine into the dough.

Johnson then left the pan of biscuits out in the open by the flame of the fire and bid his friends depart with him. It was later confirmed by another friend by the name of Jim Baker (of course he's a baker), that the intruders later returned, ate the biscuits, and perished from the poison. True or not—it seems the moral of this story is to not mess with another man's freshly cooked batch of biscuits!

The Life He Led In Final Consideration of the Crow Killer

By any modern definition, John Johnson must have been a strange man. Part vigilante, part anti-hero, and yes—part serial killing cannibal. Having said that, it is very hard to define the character of this wild man from the mountains. Part of the reason why his characteristics are so blurry to us is due to the times in which he lived.

For the frontier people in the American wilderness of the 1800s, life was hard and often brutal. Many of the tales involving John Johnson are no doubt exaggerated. But a kernel of truth is probably to be found all the same. Death was indeed a common occurrence in the wilderness terrain in which the so-called Crow Killer lived. The notion of justice was also quite different.

The idea that one would seek to take the law into their own hands and get revenge on those who had harmed their family was not too unusual in the time and place of John Johnson. Today of course, if someone so much as threatened an individual who had wronged their family, they themselves could be criminally prosecuted for even daring to make the threat.

But in John Johnson's day, the court systems and rule of law as we know it, rarely reached into the wild mountain country. The wild frontier was also not equipped with a standard police force, as all modern citizens have come to depend upon today. For the most part, folks in these wildlands were entirely on their own when it came to handling their grievances with others.

And one aspect of the Crow Killer's story that rings quite true, is the account of Johnson being part of a local posse tasked with keeping the peace. In the absence of official policing, these rough men were given authority to break up arguments and generally seek to right wrongs that had been done to community members.

In wild, untamed parts of America, before police departments, jails, and court systems could be established, this was indeed standard fare. Right or wrong, community members in these remote regions often felt that they had to take the law into their own hands and mete out justice as they saw fit. So, considering these conditions—it wouldn't come as a surprise if someone like John Johnson sought to seek out his own definition of justice against the killers of his wife and unborn child.

It seems that his wrath against his enemies earned him equal parts respect, fear, and grudging admiration. All three of these elements, combined with a hearty dose of dark and dour humor encapsulate the complicated—and yes, twisted—a life that John Johnson; the Crow Killer, must have led. And he became a larger-than-life shadow that haunted his whole community.

At any rate, even the legendary Crow Killer couldn't outlast Father Time. And it's said that by the year

1895, and by now well past middle age, John Johnson's health began to falter and fail him. He had always been robust in the past, but now he was becoming increasingly feeble. Known as an "Old Trapper," he tried to eke out what little bit of an existence he could, by skinning the pelts of small animals, but much of his previous independence began to slip away.

Even with the help of friends and neighbors, he couldn't take care of his property as well as he did in the past and ended up selling large portions of it. The last of which he sold off in 1899. He then headed west on his last journey, to what would ultimately be his final destination.

Unable to hide his wrinkles any longer, the old-timer was taken in by the so-called "Old Soldiers Home" in Los Angeles, California. He would pass away here, a short time later, on the 21st of January, in the year 1900. The Crow Killer had breathed his last, but the legends revolving around his strange and chilling exploits in the mountains would live on for over a century and longer.

Made in United States
Cleveland, OH
19 January 2025

13573294R10033